Kin Types

poems by

Luanne Castle

Finishing Line Press
Georgetown, Kentucky

Kin Types

ACKNOWLEDGMENTS

Broad Street (Forthcoming): "An Account of a Poor Oil Stove Bought off Dutch
Pete," "Half-Naked Woman Found Dead," "Once and Now," "Photo
Album Left Out for Trash," "The First Baby Still Sleeps Long Hours"

Copper Nickel: "What Came Between a Woman and Her Duties"

In Parentheses: "The Weight of Smoke"

California Journal of Poetics: "What Lies Inside"

Toasted Cheese: "And So It Goes"

Museum of Americana: "Advice from My Forebears," "The Ill-Timed Elopement"

Blast Furnace Press: "When Your Grandfather Shows You Photographs of
His Mother"

Publisher: Leah Maines
Editor: Christen Kincaid
Cover Art: Luanne Castle
Author Photo: Renee Rivers
Cover Design: Elizabeth Maines

Printed in the USA on acid-free paper.
Order online: www.finishinglinepress.com
    also available on amazon.com

Author inquiries and mail orders:
Finishing Line Press
P. O. Box 1626
Georgetown, Kentucky 40324
U. S. A.

Table of Contents

for my children Marc and Marisha
who taught me that
kinship means shared stories

and for those who came before me
whose stories I was privileged
to try to inhabit, if only for a moment

"We're all ghosts. We all carry, inside us,
people who came before us."

Liam Callanan

Advice from My Forebears

Always use hot pack canning for your green beans
and test your seals at the end.

Don't grab a burning oil stove without considering
the consequences.

Don't get in debt. If you don't got it, don't get it.

Make up your mind what church you'll attend
and go there as often as you can stand.

Be Dutch or you ain't much.

Get the log out of your own eye so you can get
the speck out of the other's eye.

We can't talk about it, but here's your great-grandma's
Eastern Star ring so you will have a signal.

Never pick a fight but if someone hits you,
hit them back.

Always plant marigolds in your vegetable garden
and keep a compost pile out beyond the shed.

If they come to your door, feed them. Then send
them on their way.

Just let be.

Be careful with a needle; that's how your Grandpa
got blinded, coming around his ma's knee.

Sit on my finger, nobody ever fell off.

Watch your step on deck so you don't fall off the boat
and get skewered by the anchor like your Uncle Lucas.

Don't quit writing like I did. Make me a promise.

Quit scowling or your face will freeze that way.

If you see somebody's thumb stuck in the dyke,
don't pull it out.

An Account of a Poor Oil Stove Bought off Dutch Pete

It is the children, their screams unwritable, unreadable, lifting skin from muscle, blood vessels, glands, cells, corpuscles. She hears them from across the yard over the fence, becomes one with the elms, the always-barking dog, the rats in the outhouse, Dirk's mare with her Sunday braid and, of course, her neighbor's children Jan and Geertruida and the youngest. Her apron blooms into billowing sail. The gate latch sticks, no match for her determined fist. Through her neighbor's petunias unseeing until at the open door regenerative flames surge from every cranny.

Under the smoke, she can make out the sliced strawberries centered on the oilcloth nailed to the tabletop.

She can't keep going, but she does. She and the fire column in movement, she forward. It spins upward a hallucinatory dance. The neighbor and her children have forgotten motion; their screams have left them behind
      swirling
        charging
          the tin ceiling
Did she take note here?
      This is the moment my life changes.
      I can't finish the dishes, wash my unmentionables,
         get dinner ready for Dirk and the children before
            it's too late. It's going to happen.
        It's happening now.

              What made a brick mason's wife, a woman with three children, the sister of three sisters and a brother, leap to a conclusion? Too late to turn back, her arms are around the stove. Human movement, it turns out, doesn't fly or sail. It's jerky and that's when she learns what she can do. Oil and flame slick and lick her limp apron, her dress, her shoes, her hands—burn away grease cotton shirting fine hairs epidermis penetrate blood vessels cells. She spots the cistern, a water-holding pit, not a well.

She jumps

Hands of all sizes reach for her. They've come from homes and businesses. Pulling her up, every touch a new agony she has yet to feel. As she rises a glistening babe, old flesh separates from unborn flesh. She stands before them peeled.

Aaltje Paak DeKorn
1852-1908
Lexmond, Zuid-Holland, Netherlands
Kalamazoo, Michigan, United States

And So It Goes

Their beginning
Pieter scrubbed before he visited Neeltje on the porch, but the oily smell of herring clung to his skin and hair, to his coat and boots. He left at ten every night. Later, she would press her hands, the ones he held as they sat turned toward each other in the small chairs, to her face and inhale. It had the effect of smelling salts or a burnt feather, reviving her from the dullness she felt when he was not around.

Their ending
When he felt invisible cold vines wrap around his ankles and calves, he saw her more clearly than he had in twenty years. His son Karel whispered that he would be seeing Mother soon. Pieter first thought he meant the mother he had never known, but then realized it was Neeltje and smiled at the image of her standing before the light.

And so it goes

On those evenings, her parents sat at the table inside the window, struggling to keep their eyes open over her mending and his reading. They didn't seem to notice when she and Pieter disappeared from view for a half hour. Or in the early months when she first let out her skirt.

He thought of his family—his children, grandchildren, and their children. His oldest great-grandchild married young, but she didn't have to. The man was older, a college graduate. Their first living room furniture was made from California orange crates, and Pieter doubted she realized her great-grandfather had ever been anything but a shrunken old man. Or that he had built chests and credenzas when Grand Rapids meant well-made furniture.

To get permission, they had to contact his mother's father, the legal guardian that had signed Pieter and his brother into the city-run orphanage four years before. Old enough to be financially responsible for himself, but not old enough to sign his own marriage license. Laws written by old men who couldn't remember their youths.

Every three months he moved to a different farmhouse. He was supposed to be with his eldest son Karel this season, but Karel's wife Clara had cancer of the womb and lay dying in the upstairs bedroom. Now he had taken ill at Pete's where the pies and fried chicken weren't as good as Clara's. But they treated him well, bringing him his pipe or a shawl when he asked for it.

She was a 16-year-old ex-schoolgirl when Karel was born. She swaddled the baby carefully, and against her mother's instructions, carried him to the dock to wait for Pieter. When he said they should leave their families and move to Kloetinge where he could learn the trade of shoemaker, her cycles stopped again. Jan was born in Kloetinge without family nearly.

Nine children born to Neeltje. Two funerals. The one he remembered in color and detail was the first, young Jan, three months old after they had arrived in Michigan. Neeltje was only 19 when she buried her second born. After that, she went some place Pieter couldn't follow. Gradually, over the next 44 years, he stopped searching.

When Pieter's wealthy grandmother passed away, his own bequest bought Pieter, Neeltje, and their two babies a voyage on the S.S. Zaandam to New York and then a train ride to Grand Rapids where other Zeeuws had moved. Their young blond family was dutifully welcomed, but without warmth, into the neighborhood. A church elder hired Pieter on at his furniture factory.

For years Pieter wondered if the sawdust and paint chemicals would harm his lungs, exposed as he'd been to first Karel's and then young Henry's tuberculosis. But he retired without incident, although his legs sometimes gave him trouble, especially in damp weather.

Neeltje's motions with the children were deliberate and patient. When she washed small faces, their eyes gazed up into hers. After Rosa died, she gave birth to yet another daughter and called her Rosa. The child they called Nellie after her mother was born slow with a pinched face and poor eyesight.

His mind wandered further back in time. The orphanage teacher with a swaggering moustache beat him across the back of his thighs with a cane after daily prayers. Afterward, Pieter found adventure stories in the Bible and imagined himself far away on another continent.

Neeltje did things without fanfare or explanation, and that's how she died. He wasn't sure what happened, but after he saw she was gone, he realized that even though she'd been at his side since they were teens, he had the sense he didn't know her. Perhaps he'd been mistaken not to try to pull her back after Jan's death. He should have tried harder. Now he envisioned her as a teen with a broad plain face, a bashful half-smile, and colorless hair. He'd made her a mother many times over, but she had been only a girl.

Pieter didn't have a photograph of his mother. As he grew up, he didn't know her stories. When Pieter was fifteen, his father died and not one of the older siblings, the uncles, or his mother's father came to save his younger brother and himself from the orphanage that resembled a dark brick church adorned with stone angels. City taxes, including those of his uncles' import business, had helped support the institution for years. The family figured they might as well make use of it.

He wanted to do it all over again. He would look often at her, at Neeltje, smiling or frowning. And at the children laughing with their mother. The smells of the fish, the leather, the fresh cut wood would be with him, but he would notice her so that when she died—because it always came to that—he would be prepared. He would see the way she was. The way they were. And it would be enough.

Pieter Philippus Mulder
1865-1953
Goes, Zeeland, Netherlands
Grand Rapids, Michigan, United States

Neeltje Gorsse Mulder
1868-1932
Goes, Zeeland, Netherlands
Grand Rapids, Michigan, United States

Baptism in the Morning

Each one grown, three girls and a son, and this year a baby all over again. That morning, when the churchwomen's eyes brimmed over with questions, she rolled her own at her husband. As she braced herself against the slow sharp slashes of shame, many-colored, their varying affect, her viscera soaked up the family guilt. Did talk idle in the wind, on the unfurled branches? She tried not to wonder what they thought. Now she glanced sideways at the tipped-down face of her eldest, brown hair bobbed and curling from the temples, eyes intent on her fingers folding back shells at the seams, peas sent popping into the bowl like children into a ceramic world. While the two younger girls milked the cow and hauled the water, the two women in the kitchen prepared dinner as if they were interchangeable, slipping a milk rag into the baby's mouth, hushing her cries, first one, then the other.

Margarethe Wendel Klein
1869-1932
Budesheim, Germany
Elmhurst, Illinois, United States

Farmhouse Table

A table big enough to hold the family of seven
and several drop-ins for roast and roots.
A pine table glazed dark, its heaviness offset
by burns and holes made by the boys' fork tines
when they tried to skewer each other's hands.
A table that displayed the family Bible brought
from home and the wild flower sketches and sums
of the children's schoolwork and Mother's sewing.
A table now invisible, draped in an old clean sheet.

Last week her husband practiced on a brindle cow.
Now he sterilizes his tools with boiling water.
Under her daughter's hips she pushes a pillow
that will have to be thrown away later. She
feels blasphemous praying, but knows the dangers.
The girl's calf-like legs splayed, and not yet a woman.
She cries piteously, a young animal sacrificed
for the family table. They have little to cut her pain
but the whiskey rag in her mouth and those in her fists.

Anonymous

Genealogy

Tigers die and leave their skins;
people die and leave their names. ~Japanese Proverb

The more relatives I unearthed,
the more Franks rose to the surface
like deer bones after a storm.
On the trails I could follow,
I found seven named Frank,
three Franz, three Francis.
Frans, Francois, and Franciscus.
Frances and Francisca,
the women peeking out
from under their fathers' names.
The name passed forward
like a cross polished by many hands.
The verb *frank* means to allow free passage
for man or post. But these Franks
and Franciskas paid with their labor
and their babes buried along the way.

Half-Naked Woman Found Dead
July 9 1920

On Thursday night last, the body of Mrs. Louisa Noffke, 73, was discovered at the shoreline of Emmons Lake by an unidentified passerby. The farm of Mrs. Noffke, a widow, abutted the lake. It appears that earlier that evening, Mrs. Noffke left her home, ripping and losing half of her clothing along the way. The blouse and stockings were not recovered. She managed to scratch and bruise herself as she trampled a path in the tall weeds, which led from the adjacent property down to the water.

Mrs. Noffke immigrated to this country from Germany with her husband and infant son when she was 25 years old. She will be interred in a metallic coffin next to her husband at Lakeview Cemetery. Her property is to be divided between her daughter Clara and her son Herman. A probate order was issued within 48 hours of her death.

The last time Mrs. Noffke can be found gracing our pages is 27 years ago when son Herman was charged with assaulting his father, the late Charles Noffke. Herman did a ghost dance around the room, then buckled into his father and, securing a grapevine lock, flopped him so hard that the jolt jarred all the plaster from the ceiling.

Herman claims it was necessary to subdue his father because "the old man" came home with his "tank full" and proceeded to make things lively. After cuffing Herman's mother, Charles Noffke kicked furniture around the room, and threw the old brindle cat through a panel of the door and "whooped her up for all he was worth."

Defying expectation, Mrs. Noffke's life got no easier when her husband died. Coroner J. B. Hilliker pronounced Mrs. Noffke's death due to indigestion.

More Burials
for Jackie Dinnis

"His good manners and genuine dutch intrepidity
in the fierce battles in which he participated had
won the admiration of his officers."
> Peter J. Haze
> Co. E, 2d Reg't. U.S. Inf.

What will happen to my youngest,
little Gerrit with the overlarge eyes,
after they bury me in the kerk cemetery?
Arie will keep him emptying pots
in the f5 rooms over the tavern, but
his catarrh might be something
more as it gets worse every night.
It may be that Arie too will die,
and my rugs and dishes auctioned.
The three eldest in different cities,
and the four young ones sent to
the orphanage at Neerbosch.
Teachers like scavengers pick
at the remains of my family,
beating Lambertus, Hermanus,
Adriana, and Gerrit himself.
I fear doubly for Adriana, knowing
the sort of men that the children's home
attracts, but Gerrit acts swiftly
and with great courage and files
a report with the police. Cornelis
de Bruin is jailed, and Adriana,
Gerrit, and the others do not return.
Lambertus packs his Bijbels
and travels to America, promising
I'll send for you to the others.

When Gerrit finally arrives to meet
his brother, they work together
printing a Dutch newspaper and
at the little market. Within a year
Gerrit hears the whistles blow
when his new country goes to war
with Spain. He drops his work
to march out to enlist. His employer
is sorry to see him go, but
impressed by his patriotism
and dignity. Gerrit is buried
twice, once in Santiago and
later near his brother in Kalamazoo.
Far from the cemetery here in
Zwammerdam, far from the hole
they have already begun to dig.

Marijtje Hoogendoorn Leeuwenhoek
1842-1878
Zwammerdam, Zuid-Holland, Netherlands
Gouda, Zuid-Holland, Netherlands

New Life, New Music

The boy in knee pants didn't notice
the many wrinkles
or if he did they created that comfortable
space between his own raw starch
and her eyes and smile that were only his.
Already her height, he spent
his days fishing and playing ball.
He thought her wide, but under the six skirts
her small frame had shriveled. She reached
under two layers and pulled out an apple,
polishing it on her apron before
presenting it to him with a magician's
flourish on the tip of her knitting needle.
His dark blond curls were so
like her brother Lucas when a baby
and not yet the young man she kissed
in his black coffin.
She and Lucas at the canal-side herring
market, listening for the bells, stealing
into the Pepperbus, Catholic
and forbidden. They played Sjoelbak
in the alley. This boy brought into
movement all these dead memories,
animating them with this new place,
each day rhythms born in them.

Jennegien Bomhoff Zuidweg
1838-1924
Zwolle, Overjissel, Netherlands
Kalamazoo, Michigan, United States

Once and Now

His letter, once wet and now dry, once
wrinkled now smoothed against her breast,
once a receptacle for all he could not say,
the lone poppy in the field, the striped sky, not
the mud, men, horses, bullets, shovels.
Definitely not, but she suspects as much.
She listens to her husband outside the church
door, reads the casualty lists, hovers around
those waiting. Now her big brother's letter
like his touch on their dying mother's cheek,
is enough. He's been long a soldier, the bachelor
patriarch. In the early days he wrote pages
of the trembling sweep of the Pacific,
ancient trees and reeds poking like magic
sticks from the water, a field of buttercups
near the Presidio, a borrowed horse he rode.
Given their immigrant circumstances, the career
had seemed wise until now, with Huns like red
devils leering down from propaganda posters
jeering them with their German names,
a town friend's Dachshund ripped from her arms,
his brains smashed on the pavement, onto
her shoes. Shoes she showed Clara, pointing,
See, see how dangerous they are in their hate!
The knock sneaks up on her from behind.
She has turned to put the letter in the ribbon-
tied stack, so standing between fourteen years
of letters and the knock, she knows that this
is not the paperboy coming for his coin.
She knows what a ridiculous leap her mind
has made, but still she is certain about the paper,

and it is a paper telegram. Without opening it,
she slips the Western Union under the grosgrain.
Once busy, she has all the time in the world now.

Clara Mulder née Waldeck
1884-1953
Caledonia, Michigan, United States

Someone Else's Story

All the ways of self-pity were open to her.
With a bitter putty she sealed each off. A wife
and mother alone with strangers, skimming
milk and scraping her knuckles on the washboard
for these middle-aged farmers and their son
almost her own age. She knelt on the floor
and scrubbed and scrubbed because she felt
too tired to stand. She avoided their eyes.
Twice when they thought she was out at the barn
she'd heard them talking about her as if she
were a cow hobbled for the sake of her calf.
That's when her story sounded to her like that
of someone else, a poor orphan in a book
she'd read in another life. Yet she was no orphan,
her mother living in the city, caring for
her grandson who still wore white dresses and ringlets.
Her story sounded harsh and chronological,
even cold. A young couple with their first baby
and no reason to think there wouldn't be more.
The husband's wagon is hit by a streetcar.
Because he's lost his wits, he's sent to the asylum
in Kalamazoo, too far to visit more than twice
a year. The young wife can only support herself
as a live-in and sends her wages to her mother.
Better not to think of these things and to study
late at night her correspondence course.
Work study work study. She was no cow.

Caroline Meier Waldeck
1872-1946
Gaines Township, Kent County, Michigan

The Fat Little House

Watch where you're pitching
an old wad of tinfoil. The sound of its
slap on the porch is hollow and supernaturally
weighty.

Who threw it? The workman
Who employed him? The septic tank company
Who employed them? The homeowners
When was the yard last dug up? When the home
was built forty years ago
What is it like now? The wood sides
of the little house are crazed,
the sidewalk and window frames cracked
and pebbling
What is its story? Start at the beginning

A sweet house, he called it.
He nailed the last of the wood
and wiped his brow with the rag
hanging from his back
pocket. But short and fat, she said
and pretended to topple the ladder.
He laughed, I like my houses like apples.
And swaddled inside the crisp
sugary walls she nurtured and nestled
babies, slippery as fruit flesh. One,
two, and then a third was lost
and a fourth born. Three children fed
in this house by her hands, by his hands.
Three children clothed in this house
by her hands and by his labors with
grease and irons. Such nourishment
went on in that fat little house,
but it couldn't sustain the one
planted in the front yard.
Most days they forgot to remember
it buried in the black soil huddled within
the tree's bony fingered roots until
it thudded onto the porch at their feet.

The First Baby Still Sleeps Long Hours

When windswept rain rattles the window panes, a draft blows out my last candle. I take good care of the taper. How will I finish my new dress in these 17-hour nights of December without light? I've thought of hemming the skirt at Christmas candle lighting, but the chintz threatens to become grubby where I've worked too long on it. If Carel hadn't been called back to run the family store, we wouldn't be moving to the provinces. I'm still wearing the dress my mother made me with the little lace shawl, a replica of her own, but I follow the new style and add my own touches—a short flowered skirt over a long plaid one. The waist is high with a long apron. With this fashion I don't need so many yards of the same fabric, but can mix patterns. Carel tries to persuade me that Goes is a big city, too, but it's not as fashionable as Middelberg, with our spectacular gothic town hall and tall merchants' homes. Carel doesn't realize I used much of the candle money to make the dress, but I can distract him in the dark. The baby still sleeps many hours in these black months. I hope to wear this dress for months before I have to let it out. No doubt another baby will be along soon, as little Jacoba arrived like a clock, and my mother said I am a young and healthy one. I suspect Carel approves of the new dress. He kisses the back of my neck when I bend over my needle. But mother scolds me, *foolish and spoiled by an ignorant husband.* If I wasn't trying to sneak time for sewing whenever possible, I'd be sleeping, nestled around Jacoba who smells of rising bread, in this gloomy season with the tang of salt and cold entering the house when the door opens. Next spring, I hope to walk the dunes, alert for nests of seabirds, before the second baby grows too burdensome.

Johanna Cornaaij Mulder
1782-1863
Middelburg, Zeeland, Netherlands
Goes, Zeeland, Netherlands

The Ill-Timed Elopement

The floral dress, ruffled and sheer, lies crushed in the cupboard under the weight of schoolbooks, laced footballs, and a catcher's mask her new husband hides from his mother. She threw books out the windows and burned them in a bonfire when disease reached her brain. Now she dies in the next room, wan and hollow in her nightgown, calling out to the young wife for compresses and water, water, more water, saying *I can't die before I see my grandchildren* and *remember to save the scraps for the dog* as she lingers in that peculiar odor of illness past blueberry season to peppers to pumpkins to the last dried husks and leaves that her son clears out with the weeds. The mother can no longer make it to the window—now closed against the dangerous air—to watch, but whispers to the wife for a cool hand on her forehead—or some garbled craziness to which the daughter-in-law is too kind to react and only wants to rescue her elopement dress and do it again in a few months when this is over.

Cora Wilhelmina DeKorn Zuidweg
1875-1932
Kalamazoo, Michigan, United States

Lucille Edna Mulder Zuidweg
1912-2000
Caledonia, Michigan, United States
Kalamazoo, Michigan, United States

The Nurturing of Nature and its Accumulations
Thank you to Behavioral Epigenetics

Anything that happened to my grandmother before she got pregnant imprinted the genes she shared with my father and then with me. Her babyhood in Budesheim, the long ship journey in steerage with the heaving crowd, learning English and forgetting German by age five. Her parents didn't know about DNA sequencing. Or how neuron activity would alter her brain. Or that these changes would be passed down. Nobody knew. Not her father who refused to let her leave the house for school after 3rd grade and responded to his children with reliable unpredictability. Not her mother who accepted his dominion. Or her older sister who left her children behind as she departed through the upstairs window. Not the doctor who falsified the sister's manner of death. Or her younger sister who refused to work because she dated a lawyer, forcing my grandmother to sew twelve hours a day in a sweatshop without benefit of spectacles. Not the doctor who treated her female dysfunction and then overstayed his welcome, fathering and delivering that gene-encoded baby boy who would become my father. Nobody knew about these matters when my father forced me to stand in the corner until I fainted. But then nobody knew that when my grandmother's father's two baby sisters died one Christmas the event would encode his genes. Genes already stricken with ages-old infections and the courage necessary for it all.

Maria Anna Elisabetha Klein
3 April 1893 Budesheim, Hessen, Germany
25 April 1974 Kalamazoo, Michigan, United States

The Weight of Smoke
1902 September 3
Kalamazoo, Michigan

The residence of George Paake at 1016 Trimble Avenue was burned this morning about 10:30 o'clock and a worthy family which has had a series of disasters, left without a home.

Kalamazoo Gazette

Fourteen-year-old Cora carried one side of her mother's favorite dresser, while her father, balancing more of the weight himself, walked backward as fast as possible. The rattle in his chest barely slowed George as he set down the piece and rushed back into the smoke-filled house. Cora's gaze lingered on the dresser before she followed him. Her guilt seemed to flow out the seams of the closed drawers. Its debris curled up like sawdust in the notches of the leaf pattern carving.

Cora Paake

Tracy and Fannie clung to Jennie who held little George in her thin arms. Her father had yelled that the only help he needed from her was to keep the three smallest from the fire. From the chimney in the column of smoke, a fan seemed to rise, unfolding its flames. Jennie tried not to see it as triumphant. She glanced down at Tracy who had stopped crying. The girl's molten eyes hardened like blown glass into marbles.

Jennie Paake

The house which Mr. Paake was paying for in the Building and Loan Association was entirely ruined although most of the contents of the home were saved. Mr. Paake receives no insurance whatever and the little which had been accumulated by the family was lost.

Kalamazoo Gazette

With the furniture assembled on the side of the street, alongside the children and a few neighbors, George watched the remains of the house burn. The thought of his dead wife's watch in the dresser drawer bobbed on the surface of his mind even as smoke escaped into the sky. He retrieved it without caring who noticed and slipped it into his pocket. Who knew what would happen to the furniture. And where would he and the children go? It was his fault for being sick in bed.

George Paake

The fire is only an incident in the history of the family. Mrs. Paake died a short time ago leaving five children, the oldest being fourteen years old. Since the mother's death the little girl has had entire charge of the house and the four little children and has had all the responsibility of the family except the support which Mr. Paake gave as a laborer. Recently he has been unable to work and was ill this morning when the fire occurred.

Kalamazoo Gazette

It replicated itself into a chain of thinking: If he hadn't been in bed. If he hadn't been ill again today. And still he coughed. Such heaviness had been placed on Cora for the past two years. As the flames disappeared and the smoke decreased, they all witnessed the end and its beginnings. He turned to seek out Cora. Her face reminded him of the way his wife used to starch the girls' white blouses and pinafores—white and unyielding. That's when he realized that since her passing, they wore soft and wrinkled dresses, now smudged with black. The front of Cora's apron had ripped. George went to her and slipped the watch on its gold chain over her neck. He should have given it to her before the fire.

George Paake

She felt his thumbs on the side of her neck and then the stone-like weight of the watch as it rolled down to dangle at the bottom of its chain. What was this? A reward for letting the house catch fire? She rubbed the smooth gold, feeling the engraved flower under her fingertips. What was beautiful to the sight felt like a flaw to the touch. More neighbors arrived, but they said the house was too far gone to save. That too was her fault for not noticing the smell of smoke after breakfast.

Cora Paake

The neighbors have taken in the little ones and are doing all that is possible to alleviate the sufferings of the family. Mrs. Carrier has been responsible for raising a sum of money to which the neighbors have liberally contributed.

Kalamazoo Gazette

Mrs. Carrier, a 68-year-old widow, who lived two streets over, got out of her carriage and bustled over to George. Somebody had to get them started and she vowed to collect a nest egg for the Paakes who now had nothing. Fannie would go with Jennie to the next door neighbors. Tracy's childless Sunday School teacher led her away. Jennie noted the girl didn't look back, though she herself couldn't bear to turn her back on the chaos in the yard.

Jennie Paake

The couple at the corner carried off young George, promising a confectioner's sugar cookie. George had seen where the matches had burned a hole in the floor, near the window where the curtains had hung. He had not told anyone. He never would. After all, no sense any of the children feeling bad over the fire when he was the one who had been lying in bed sick.

George Paake

What Came Between A Woman and Her Duties
14 May 1897

On this Friday, in our fair city of Kalamazoo, Recreation Park refreshment proprietor, John Culver, has applied to the Circuit Court to gain custody of his two young daughters from his divorced wife. The girls currently reside in the Children's Home. They were accompanied to court by Miss Bradley, the matron of the home.

Mrs. Culver, the divorcée, and the children were represented by J. W. Adams. The father was represented by F.E. Knappen. Mrs. Culver, pale and stern-looking, wore a shirtwaist with tightly ruched collar and generous mutton sleeves. The strain of her situation shows clearly on her visage. In the past, Mrs. Culver has been aided and abetted by her female friends in the art of painting, as an article of 6 February 1895 in this very daily can attest.

A large number of friends of both parties were in the courtroom and heard emotional pleadings on both sides. Judge Buck ascertained that Mrs. Culver is engaged in the pursuit of an honest living at this time and so ordered that the children remain in the mother's care. She was given six months to bring them home from the orphanage or they will go into the care of their father and his mother. Let us hope that Mrs. Culver can stay away from the easel.

What Lies Inside

Outside the fence the street leans down town past
    wood and brown shingled storefronts and homes.
  I can drive my trap or walk, but I prefer to stay put
    where they can't steal from me.
Inside the fence, I count. Black and white cat with her sucklings:
    one, two, three, four.
  Stable with carriage and two horses, chicken coop,
    shed, front stoop. We sit tiered by generation.

Outside the house my father signed the dark brick
    with light stone bands, as a parcel is tied with twine.
  He is known throughout the county for his masonry.
    I expect my end to meet my beginning here.
Inside, my father's pipe smoke circles him as a frame defines
    its subject. My husband locks the store late
and comes home to a dinner plate-sized steak, business
    talk with my father, a bottle of jenever.

Outside the door with its tulip carving my little son crowds
    me, pulls my skirt, raises his arms to me
palms open. I close them in my fists, turn away. What heavy air,
    close with tobacco and burnt meat.
What lies inside is one bed, one dresser, one washstand and my husband
    damp and rosy reaching for me, too.
  If I don't have this one space, where can I go to protect this self
    kept inside only by my thin twitching skin?

What lies outside my mind is nothing. Mother's bones cleaner
    than steak bones, buildings diminish to the horizon.

Inside my mind
a junkyard, castoffs from outside others,
    flickering and igniting when struck on its inside walls.

Cora Wilhelmina DeKorn Zuidweg
1875-1932
Kalamazoo, Michigan, United States

When Your Grandfather Shows You Photographs of His Mother

You identify yourself in the antique image. Long slender neck, narrow torso, your face tipped to avoid the light. Your hands rest in the valley between your thighs sharp under yards of stiff calico. Your face long, well-sculpted by a lean diet and youth, nearly but not ascetic. Blue veins clutch the temples under translucent skin, a milky film that just contains you. In the next photograph your black dog Carlo poses at your side.

But Carlo isn't your dog. Three degrees separate you across the time dimension. You never beat a man with his horse-whip for using it on his horse, though you wish you had that sort of courage and that sort of hands-on life, or burned all the books except the family Bible, praise her lord. And yet you hold your bodies as both shields and thresholds.

Because a face never reflects the same, every photo sees something else. You're your father under the red star and your mother's grandmother in the morning sun. But not your mother who is the image of her aunt. You never did let her kiss you. You see Carlo and his mistress in another photograph, and her smile is so familiar. Now the gauzy mask of your mother's face floats across her-your features. Another light source and hour. Another shift of the hologram that is you.

Cora Wilhelmina DeKorn Zuidweg
1875-1932
Kalamazoo, Michigan, United States

W inner of the 2015 New Mexico-Arizona Book Award, *Doll God*, **Luanne Castle**'s first collection of poetry, was published by Aldrich Press. Luanne's poetry and prose have appeared in *Grist, Copper Nickel, River Teeth, Glass Poetry Press, Barnstorm Journal, Six Hens, Lunch Ticket, The Review Review*, and many other journals.

Luanne has been a Fellow at the Center for Ideas and Society at the University of California, Riverside. She studied English and creative writing at the University of California, Riverside (Ph.D.); Western Michigan University (MFA); and the Stanford University writing certificate program. Her scholarly work has been published in academic journals, and she contributed to *Twice-Told Children's Tales: The Influence of Childhood Reading on Writers for Adults*, edited by Betty Greenway. For fifteen years, she taught college English.

An avid blogger, Luanne can be found at luannecastle.com. She divides her time between California and Arizona, where she shares land with a herd of javelina.

CPSIA information can be obtained
at www.ICGtesting.com
Printed in the USA
LVOW11s2350080817
544306LV00001B/21/P